Gaming and eSports

# WARP ZONE

## THE FUTURE OF GAMING

Kaitlyn Duling

Rourke Educational Media

A Division of Carson Dellosa Education

# BEFORE AND DURING READING ACTIVITIES

## Before Reading: *Building Background Knowledge and Vocabulary*

Building background knowledge can help children process new information and build upon what they already know. Before reading a book, it is important to tap into what children already know about the topic. This will help them develop their vocabulary and increase their reading comprehension.

### Questions and Activities to Build Background Knowledge:

1. Look at the front cover of the book and read the title. What do you think this book will be about?
2. What do you already know about this topic?
3. Take a book walk and skim the pages. Look at the table of contents, photographs, captions, and bold words. Did these text features give you any information or predictions about what you will read in this book?

### Vocabulary: *Vocabulary Is Key to Reading Comprehension*

Use the following directions to prompt a conversation about each word.

- Read the vocabulary words.
- What comes to mind when you see each word?
- What do you think each word means?

**Vocabulary Words:**
- *adaptive*
- *cloud*
- *diverse*
- *immersive*
- *scholarship*
- *streaming*

## During Reading: *Reading for Meaning and Understanding*

To achieve deep comprehension of a book, children are encouraged to use close reading strategies. During reading, it is important to have children stop and make connections. These connections result in deeper analysis and understanding of a book.

 ### Close Reading a Text

During reading, have children stop and talk about the following:

- Any confusing parts
- Any unknown words
- Text to text, text to self, text to world connections
- The main idea in each chapter or heading

Encourage children to use context clues to determine the meaning of any unknown words. These strategies will help children learn to analyze the text more thoroughly as they read.

When you are finished reading this book, turn to the next-to-last page for **After-Reading Questions** and an **Activity**.

# Table of Contents

Level Up .................................................... 4
New Ways to Play ...................................... 6
Playing to Win! ......................................... 12
Games for All ............................................ 18
Gaming for Good ...................................... 24
Memory Game .......................................... 30
Index .......................................................... 31
After-Reading Questions ......................... 31
Activity ...................................................... 31
About the Author ..................................... 32

# LEVEL UP

Fasten your seat belts. We are now entering the time-warp tunnel. Once inside, you'll get a glimpse of the future. The future of video gaming, that is! People have been plugging in to play for nearly a century. In that time, games have advanced at super speeds. Today's games look nothing like those of the 1950s and '60s—or even the games of the '90s and early 2000s!

So, what games will your kids and grandkids play? What will video games look like in the next 100 years? It's time to find out. Hold on tight. It could be a bumpy ride!

# NEW WAYS TO PLAY

## AR

Video game designers agree—the future of video games isn't on a TV screen. It's not on a tablet or smartphone screen. No, the video games of the future will put the game into the real world. In augmented reality, or AR, computer-generated objects, characters, and other elements enhance the physical world.

In the popular *Pokémon Go!* game, you use a smartphone to "catch" Pokémon in your backyard or bedroom. In the future, you may be able to play AR ping-pong on your kitchen counter. Or you might fly a rocket through the house!

## AR EVERYWHERE

Developers are working on AR for everyday tasks. Someday, you might "try on" clothes in a virtual dressing room or use AR to redecorate your bedroom with virtual furniture

If AR means putting the game into your world, then virtual reality, or VR, is the opposite. In VR games, players enter a 3D world. These games often use goggles or headsets. The games trick your brain into thinking the virtual world is real.

Can you imagine a screen that takes up your entire field of vision? Instead of your living room, you might see a spooky forest or an arena. You can walk through the space and interact with the characters. That's what VR feels like.

In the future, some games might take it a step further. They will allow you to become the game, no controller needed! Intel RealSense technology lets players control games using gestures. It learns movements. This allows for very **immersive** gameplay.

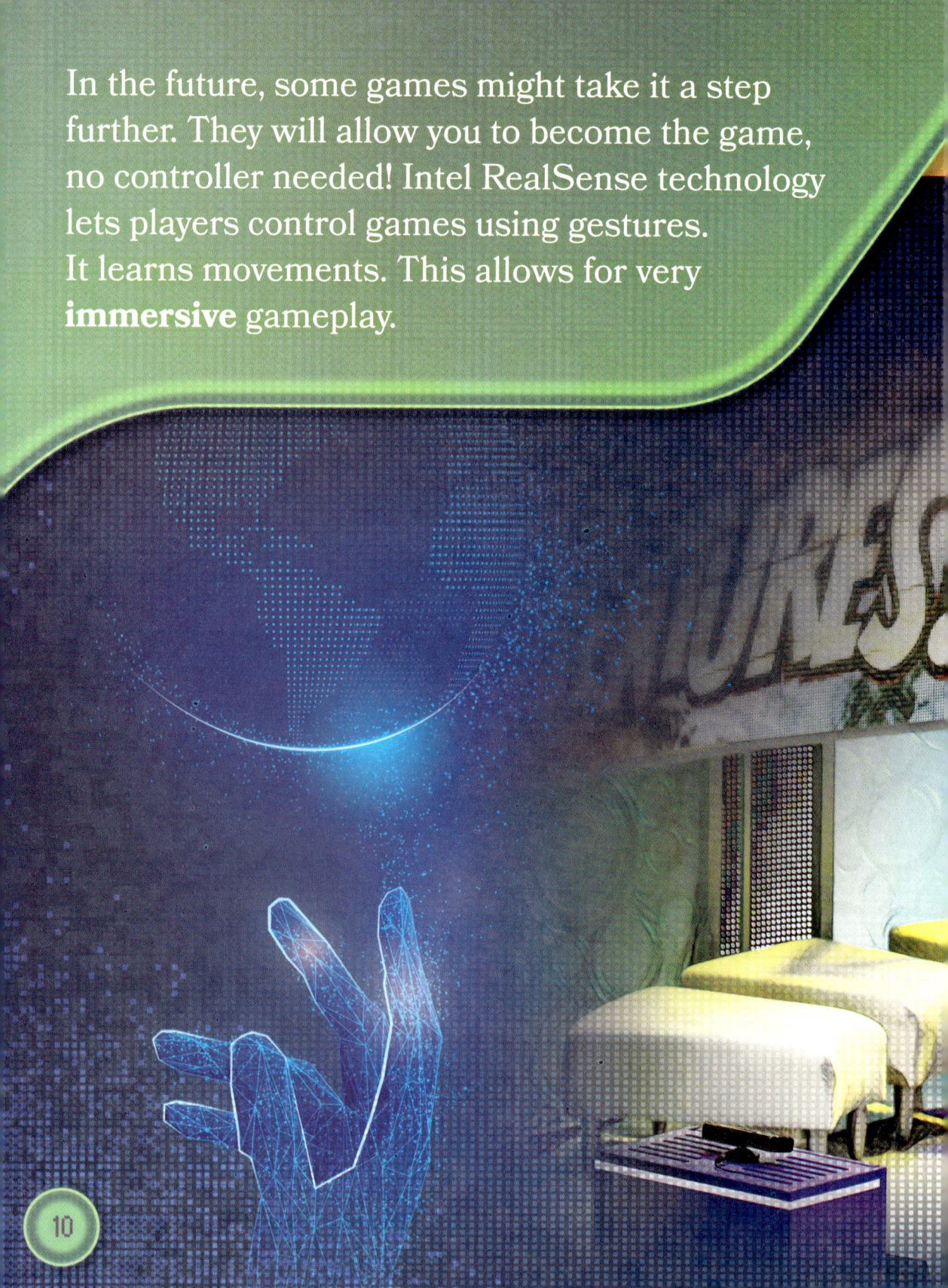

**IMMERSIVE** (i-MURS-iv): deeply engaging

## PLAYING WITH YOUR EMOTIONS

Someday, we might play games with our feelings. Companies are working on games that recognize players' faces and voices.

# PLAYING TO WIN!

With the rise of AR and VR, video games are getting more creative—and more physical. Games of the future could blend physical sports with 3D effects. Imagine playing soccer with a team of unicorns or catching a bug instead of a baseball!

Competitive gaming will certainly look different in the future. In fact, it's already starting to change. These days, popular and competitive video games are called eSports. They have teams, fans, and huge championships.

　We all know that video games can be expensive. Lucky for some, today's game champs can get paid to play. Dozens of colleges in the United States are offering eSports **scholarships**. With good grades and high scores, students can play their way onto a college team.

　The University of California, Irvine even built a campus gaming arena! UCI gamers (called Anteaters) play on a fleet of 72 computers. In the future, more schools are expected to offer eSports teams.

> **SCHOLARSHIPS** (SKAH-lur-ships): money given to go to college or follow a course of study

## GOLD MEDAL GAMES

The Olympics could someday include eSports. The 2024 Olympics in Paris will feature some demo gaming events. It's up to the International Olympic Committee to decide if any video games will officially join the Olympics.

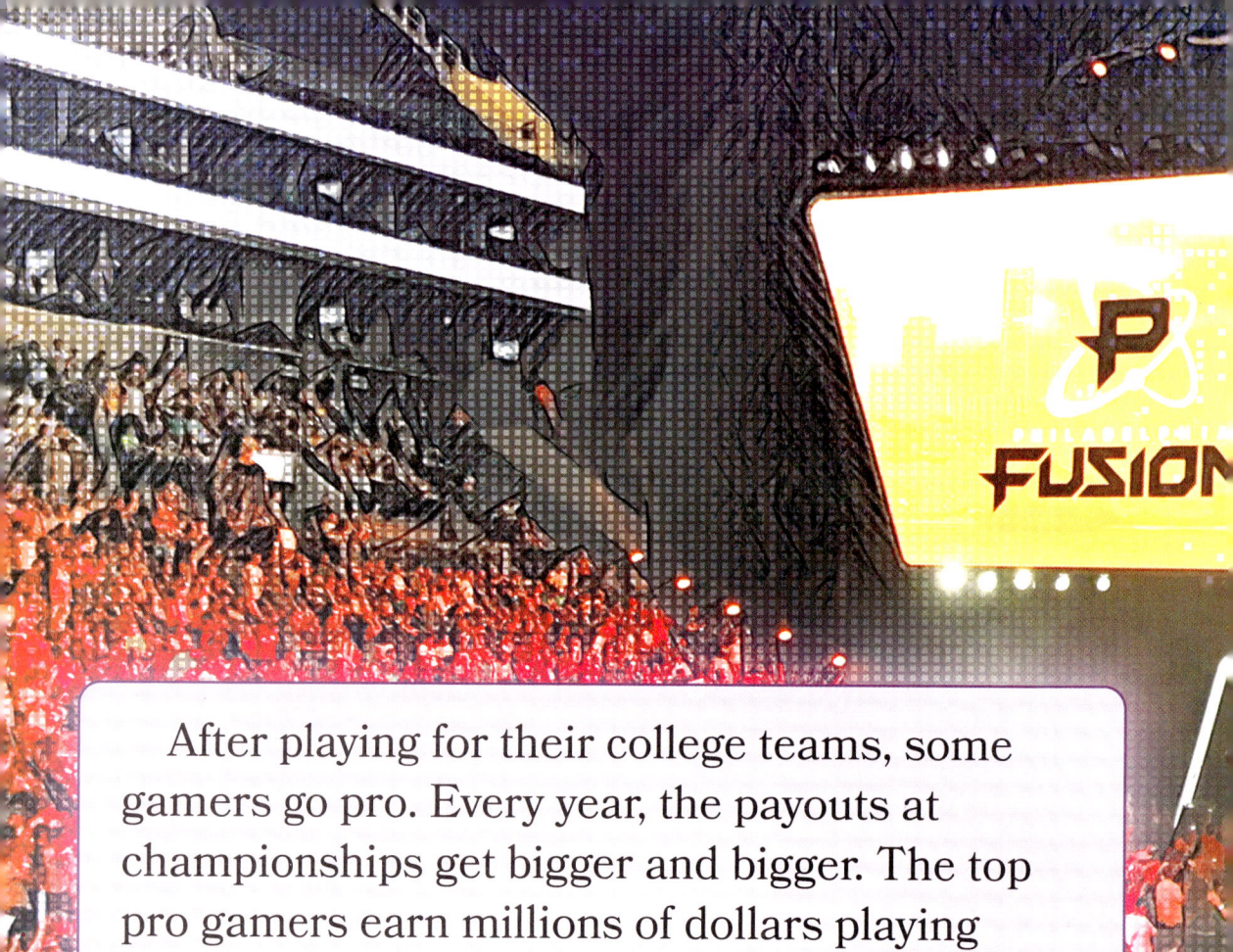

After playing for their college teams, some gamers go pro. Every year, the payouts at championships get bigger and bigger. The top pro gamers earn millions of dollars playing games like *Dota 2*, *Fortnite*, and *Counter-Strike: Global Offensive*. In the coming years, they can expect to earn even more.

As the payouts for eSports get bigger, some gamers may see more opportunities to cheat. In 2021, a *League of Legends* team was found guilty of "screen-peeking" at a championship. The team was fined 12% of their earnings—$30,000!

## HAT TIP:

You'll NEVER see an e-Sports pro wearing a hat at a live event. Competitions often ban hats. They can help gamers cheat! A gamer could move their headset under the hat and listen-in to rivals.

# GAMES FOR ALL

Over the years, video gaming has only become more popular. According to one recent study, three out of every four people in the U.S. play video games! That's about 244 million people. When we look to the future of video gaming, it's likely we'll see more and more people plugging in. That means the gaming world will have to get a little bigger. Luckily, it's already on its way.

Video games have slowly but surely become more **diverse**. Women, people of color, and people with disabilities are starting to see themselves in new games. *The Sims 4* is just one example of games that are adding more skin tones and hairstyles.

**DIVERSE** (dye-VURS): having many different types or kinds

## THIS GAME ROCKS

*Stacks On Stacks (On Stacks)* is a new game featuring Rockit, a young girl on a big adventure. It was important to the creators that their game have a Black girl with natural hair at its center. When more people can see themselves in video games, the gaming community grows. We all win!

Some of the coolest new tools and features in gaming are **adaptive**. These tools help people play games with ease. For example, the SUBPAC M2X is a wearable vest for hearing-impaired gamers. It turns game audio into thumps and vibrations that the player can feel. Xbox has created its own adaptive controller with larger buttons and room for additional controls. It has an adapter that can be plugged into a power wheelchair!

Another adaptive tool is Quadstick, a mouth-activated joystick for people with limited mobility. There are even some audio-only games that are perfect for gamers who have limited or no sight.

> **ADAPTIVE** (uh-DAP-tiv): able to work in a different way or change based on the situation.

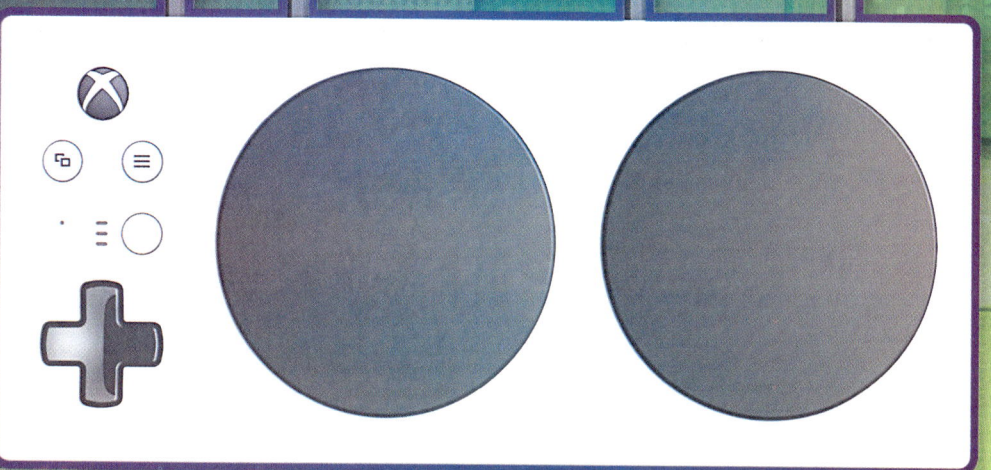

Microsoft Xbox and Windows 10 Adaptive Controller

## A NEW WAY TO MINE

EyeMine technology is a new software built for *Minecraft*. The software tracks eye movements, allowing gamers to play *Minecraft* with their eyes.

You play Nintendo Switch games on the Nintendo Switch. You play Xbox games on the Xbox. But in the future, you may be able to play any game on any device! Many experts think this technology isn't far off.

Instead of buying the latest console and the games to go with it, gamers could subscribe to a streaming service. Instead of being stored on a memory card or console, games will be saved and stored in the cloud. The **cloud** is accessed online. One of the best parts of "cloud gaming" is that it would allow more people to play at a time. Right now, many online games are capped at 100 players. With the cloud, you could have any number of people playing one game.

**CLOUD** (kloud): the computers and connections supporting online data storage

The Google Stadia is a cloud gaming service.

## ANY TIME IS GAME TIME

Do you play video games on your phone? The team at Razer is hoping their controller will help gamers level-up their mobile play. The Razer Kishi is a two-part controller that attaches to almost any smartphone. It's big-time gameplay in a small device.

# GAMING FOR GOOD

Video games are fun. They can also be exciting, interesting, and even scary! But many programmers hope the video games of the future will serve a bigger purpose. They will do good.

What will doing good look like? Some of the latest games offer a great example. *Antura and the Letters* is a free mobile game that provides education in Arabic. It hopes to reach Syrian children in refugee camps who cannot attend school. *That Dragon, Cancer* is a unique game that tells the story of a young boy diagnosed with cancer. The creators hope other families will identify with their story and find some comfort in the game.

Over the last few years, video games have moved from the living room to the classroom. There's no stopping the trend now! Flight games teach would-be pilots how to fly airplanes. People are using *Rocksmith* to learn guitar and *Duolingo* to learn different languages.

Teachers are finding that games can be used in schools. *Assassin's Creed* is used in high schools to teach history. *Roblox* and *Minecraft* help teach team building and engineering. Some teachers even use a game called *Kerbal Space Program* to help their students learn the basics of rocket science! What could be next? If you can learn it, you can game it.

## QUICK, TELL YOUR PARENTS

Recent data shows that playing video games can be good for your health! In addition to lowering stress and helping you make decisions, games may be able to improve your eyesight and keep your memory sharp. Now that's good news for gamers!

Gaming certainly has the potential to change our lives for the better. In the future, we can expect to see a wide variety of games that help us learn and grow. With new technologies like VR and AR that bring gaming to life, the games of the future will take learning to a whole new level.

Better add some sunglasses to your video game character the future of gaming and eSports is brighter than ever!

# MEMORY GAME

Look at the pictures. What do you remember reading on the pages where each image appeared?

# INDEX

3D 8, 12
augmented reality (AR) 6, 7, 8, 12, 28
cloud 22
college 14, 15, 16
competition 17
disabilities 18
learning 28
smart phone 6
pro gamer(s) 16
eSports 12, 14, 16, 28
technology 10, 21, 22
virtual reality (VR) 8, 12, 28

# AFTER-READING QUESTIONS

1. Why is diversity in gaming important?

2. What are three ways that the video game world is opening up to more people?

3. How can adaptive tools help people play video games?

4. How are eSports becoming more like traditional sports?

5. Is it possible to earn money playing video games?

# ACTIVITY

When it comes to creating video games, we are only limited by our imaginations! Think of a brand-new video game that kids could play someday. It might run on technology that hasn't been invented yet—that's okay! Write about your game idea and draw a picture to go with it. You never know, you may have just created the next hit game.

# ABOUT THE AUTHOR

Kaitlyn Duling is a lifelong lover of video games. She enjoys games that get her moving, thinking, and dreaming. When she's not on her Nintendo Switch, Kaitlyn is writing and living in Washington, DC. She has authored over 100 books for kids and teens.

© 2022 Rourke Educational Media

All rights reserved. No part of this book may be reproduced or utilized in any form or by any means, electronic or mechanical including photocopying, recording, or by any information storage and retrieval system without permission in writing from the publisher.

www.rourkeeducationalmedia.com

PHOTO CREDITS ©: page 4: coffeekai/ Getty Images; page 4: yackers1 / Shutterstock.com; page 4: Andrew Parsons GDA Photo Service/Newscom; page 5: HeliRy/ Getty Images; page 5: Nata-Lia/ Shutterstock.com; page 5: Craig Russell / Shutterstock.com; page 5: Pixls / Shutterstock.com; page 5: Boumen Japet / Shutterstock.com; page 5: Pinkasevich / Shutterstock.com; page 5: Just_Super/ Getty Images; page 7: Anton Shaparenko/ Shutterstock.com; page 7: Gorodenkoff/ Shutterstock.com; page 8: Ron Dale/ Shutterstock.com; page 9: KDdesignphoto/ Shutterstock.com; page 10: Jackie Niam/ Getty Images; page 11: MARIO ANZUONI/REUTERS/Newscom; page 12: GDA Photo Service/Newscom; page 13: Scott Wilson/ZUMA Press/Newscom; page 13: ohishiistk/ Getty Images; page 14: Budrul Chukrut/ SOPA Images/Sip/Newscom; page 16: Courtney Becker/TNS/Newscom; page 19: Sergey Novikov/ Shutterstock.com; page 19: Imagentle/ Shutterstock.com; page 20: Microsoft/Cover Images/Newscom; page 21: mkfilm/ Shutterstock.com; page 21: Microsoft/Cover Images/Newscom; page 21: ART PAL/ Shutterstock.com; page 22: Jackie Niam/ Getty Images; page 22: filo/ Getty Images; page 22: Bismillah_bd/ Getty Images; page 23: Mr.Mikla/ Shutterstock.com; page 23: Jackie Niam/ Getty Images; page 25: gn8/ Getty Images; page 25: klyaksun/ Getty Images; page 25: YakobchukOlena/ Getty Images; page 26: mkfil/ Shutterstock.com; page 26: Kashtanowww/ Shutterstock.com; page 27: Phoenix 1319/ Shutterstock.com; page 27: ART PAL/ Shutterstock.com; page 27: ymphotos/ Shutterstock.com; page 29: Prostock-studio/ Shutterstock.com; n/a: amtitus/ Getty Images

Edited by: Jennifer Doyle
Cover design and illustration by: Joshua Janes
Interior design and illustrations by: Joshua Janes

Library of Congress PCN Data

Warp Zone The Future Of Gaming / Kaitlyn Duling
 (Gaming and eSports)
 ISBN 978-1-73164-931-7 (hard cover)
 ISBN 978-1-73164-879-2 (soft cover)
 ISBN 978-1-73164-983-6 (e-Book)
 ISBN 978-1-73165-035-1 (e-Pub)
Library of Congress Control Number: 2021935476

Rourke Educational Media
Printed in the United States of America
06-1452413123